The Bible in a Nutshell & Atheisting 101

Written by Casper Rigsby

with

Illustrations by Pixelegion

Copyright © 2019 Casper Rigsby & Kelly Pitner
In association with and produced by Anti-Social Media &
Pixelegion.
All rights reserved.

TABLE OF CONTENTS

Introduction 1
The Bible in a Nutshell 2
    Introduction 4
    The Bible in a Nutshell (Part 1) 5
    Interlude (Part 1) 9
    The Bible in a Nutshell (part 2) 13
    Interlude (Part 2) 16
    The Bible in a Nutshell (Part 3) 20
    Extras & Deleted Scenes 24
    A Final Thought from Your Resident Heretic 28
Atheisting 101 29
    Introduction 31
    Part 1 32
        Step 1: Don't Believe in Gods 33
        Step 2: Worship Satan 35
        Step 3: Eat a Baby 38
        Step 4: Orgies! Orgies! Orgies! 40
        Step 5: Murder & Rape People as Much as You Want.. 42
        Step 6: Wage War Against Christmas Jesus 44
        Step 7: Worship Richard Dawkins 46
        Step 8: Free PhD! 48
        Step 9: Embrace Reality 51

Step 10: See Step 1 52
Part 2 53
A note from the author 57
About the Author 58

INTRODUCTION

I wrote both of these titles back in 2015. I wrote them in a time when things felt calm enough that religion seemed like the truly big problem I needed to focus on and I could have some fun doing that by writing these satirically silly little books. It's a bit harder lately to write a book that has some humor and all of myself without just being an angry tirade that isn't really fun or funny for anyone. So since I needed to republish these titles anyway (no comment), I thought I would throw them together as one fun and funny little treat you can throw on your coffee table to get some arguments started! Did I say arguments? I meant conversations… loud and angry conversations.

Have fun folks, and try not to murder each other because that is a dick move like at least 90% of the time.

THE BIBLE IN A NUTSHELL

The unbelievable tale of an extra-dimensional wizard and his exploits with humanity

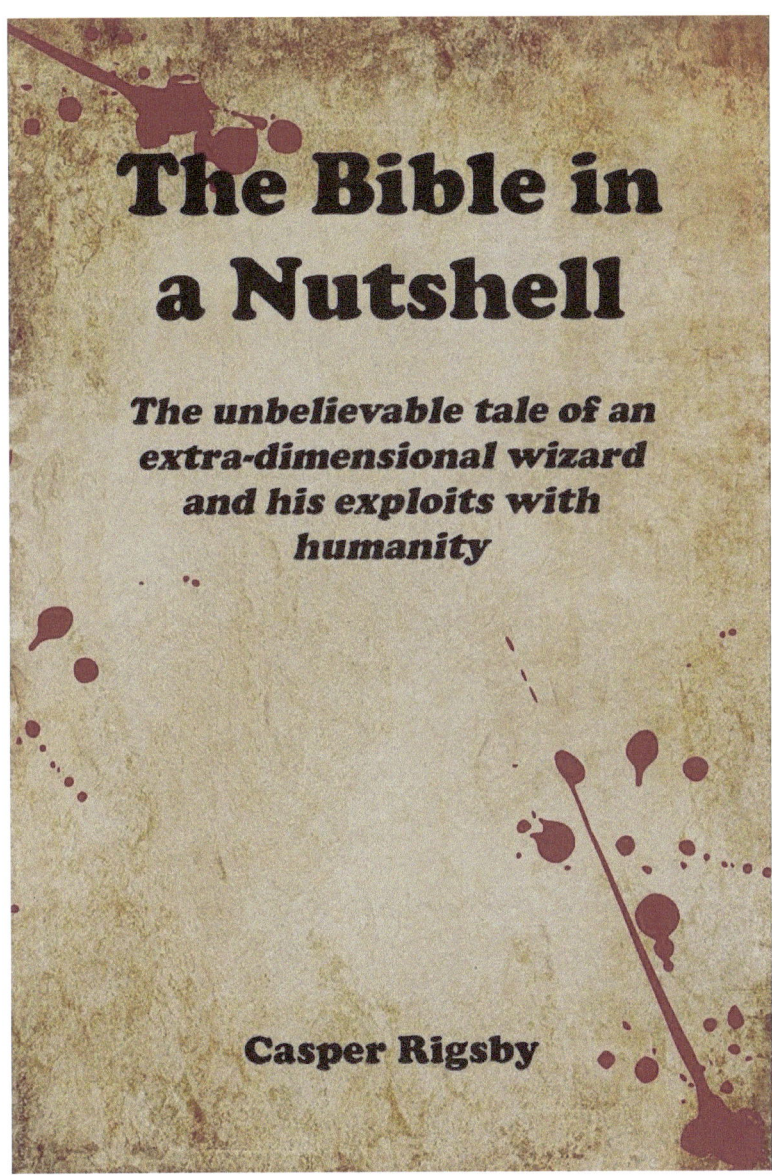

INTRODUCTION

If you've ever read the whole Bible you are well aware of just how big this book is. With an estimated word count of well over 700,000 words, the book is not an undertaking for the casual reader. In addition to the lengthiness of the book it can also be a very tedious and boring read as well. This turns many people off to wanting to commit any time to understanding the foundational doctrine of Christianity.

However, as atheists we really need to have at least a basic understanding of the Bible if we are going to make a judgment call about the religion. You see, no matter which sect of Christianity someone subscribes to the Bible is the foundation of Christian belief. So what I offer here is a mere 7,000 words to tell a slimmed down version of the basic story of the Bible. I've tried to make it humorous and something that could be fun to read.

I've stripped away all the philosophy and metaphor and simply offered the story as it is in its most basic form. Because of this, what I offer here is more a literary critique and artistic rendering than a theological examination. What I want to focus on is the narrative rather than any underlying allegory or metaphor inherent in the narrative. And what I want the reader to ask themselves is if this story is actually believable or not. I want to challenge the notion of biblical literalism by showing the story in its most basic form is simply too fantastic for any rational person to believe it as fact.

You see, if the story broken down to its most basic form doesn't make sense, it won't make more sense if you just complicate it by throwing in even more outrageous claims. I think by the time the reader finishes this story they will come to an understanding of just how silly biblical literalism truly is.

THE BIBLE IN A NUTSHELL (PART 1)

Some people have said the Bible is the greatest story ever told. I'm pretty sure that's because they haven't heard it told correctly.

Forward

What I'm going to offer here is a bit of blasphemy, or at least in the eyes of Christians it is. This is the story of the Bible broken down into sheer simplicity. Broken down and simplified in this manner it becomes abundantly apparent just how ridiculous the whole thing is. I hope you enjoy.

In The Beginning

In an alternate dimension outside of space and time lives the most powerful wizard ever known. He's so powerful that he can speak things into existence. One day he is sitting around bored and thinks, "Let me make myself some other beings that can bask in the glory of how awesome I am." So he spent six days thinking and speaking the whole universe and everything in it into existence. Then he took a nap, because that was a lot of talking to do.

One of the many things the wizard, let's call him The Wiz, created was people. He made people extra special out of dirt like a mud golem to look and think like him. Basically like little The Wiz dolls. But at first it's just this one dude named Adam and he's very lonely and bored. So The Wiz rips out one of Adam's ribs and says, "Alakadabra!" and the rib turns into another person. But this person has nipples that actually serve a purpose.

So The Wiz sets these two up with a sweet little place in a garden with everything they could ever need and then says,

"Oh, by the way, I created a tree in that garden that will kill you. Just to spice things up a bit, ya know. Don't eat the fruit off that tree."

Well one day a talking snake shows up and sees the person with the functioning nipples, her name was Eve, and says, "You simply **must** try the fruit on that one tree! It's divine!" So she does and she shares it with Adam because it's very tasty and instead of dying they just get smarter and notice they're naked. So they hide when The Wiz comes back around, because of being naked and all, and The Wiz immediately knows something is wrong. So he says, "What the fuck guys? I told you not to eat that fruit. Now I'm going to have to kick you out of the garden."

So they get kicked out and The Wiz is double pissed at Eve so he makes her menstruate and makes childbirth really painful for her. They have two boys named Cain and Abel, which end up fighting because The Wiz likes meat better than vegetables and Cain kills Abel. So The Wiz sends Cain to live in some weird land called Nod and he finds a wife there and does his thing. In the meantime, Adam and Eve have many more children and a couple thousand years go by in which the earth fills up with people.

When it Rains it Pours

Now it's thousands of years later and for some reason no one is worshipping The Wiz, which really makes him angry since he made these people specifically to glorify himself. There's this one guy named Noah though who still thinks The Wiz is super awesome. So The Wiz tells Noah, "Build a big boat and put two of every animal on the boat along with your family because I'm fixing to drown all these other assholes." Noah builds the boat and the animals come. He packs up his family and then The Wiz sets about flooding the whole world and drowning everyone. POOF - now you're a corpse. Neat trick.

After about a month and a half, once The Wiz was sure everyone was good and dead, he makes the flood waters recede some and Noah sends a dove who fetches a branch from a tree that somehow withstood the torrential floods and let's Noah know there is land ho. Noah lands the boat on a mountain, because screw you physics, he's got a wizard for a bff. Then The Wiz pops a rainbow into the sky and tells Noah that this is a sign that he won't murder everyone in that particular fashion again, because The Wiz likes to keep you guessing.

So Noah and his family repopulate the earth (let's try to gloss over the incest part). Eventually this guy Abraham comes on the scene and The Wiz really takes a liking to this dude. The Wiz tells Abraham that he's doing a super awesome job worshipping The Wiz, but unfortunately Abraham is going to need to murder his son Isaac because The Wiz likes blood. Abraham says, "Sure thing", and proceeds to carry this out. At the last minute The Wiz sends one of his personal minions to stop Abraham and tell him that The Wiz was just pranking him. Haha! Almost made you kill your kid!

Turn by Turn Mis-navigation

So we flash forward a bit more and one of Abraham's descendants named Moses gets tossed in a basket and thrown into a river. He floats to Egypt and gets found by some of pharaoh's folks who think he's cute and adopt him. But it turns out that Pharaoh has captured all the descendants of Abraham called the Jews and enslaved them. When Moses grows up and realizes he's a Jew, The Wiz tells him that Pharaoh needs to let these people go. The Wiz tells Moses to go to Pharaoh and ask him to release the Jews, but when Moses does this The Wiz has put Pharaoh under hypnosis or something and Pharaoh refuses. So The Wiz sends plagues and murders all the firstborn in Egypt to teach Pharaoh not to fall for The Wiz using magic to make him intentionally obstinate.

Eventually Moses gets all the Jews out of Egypt, but Pharaoh sends troops after them. They get to the Red Sea and they're stuck, but then Moses says, "The Wiz taught me a trick" and he pounds a walking stick on the ground. The sea splits in two and all the Jews walk over to the other side. The Egyptian troops try to follow them and The Wiz makes the sea fall back on them and drown them. POOF - now you're a corpse. (That trick is getting old)

So now Moses and the Jews are free and The Wiz tells them he has a special place for them to live. But before they can get there Moses has a one on one with The Wiz and is given a bunch of rules for how to properly worship The Wiz. When Moses goes to tell all the Jews the new rules, they've made a cow out of gold and are worshipping it.... because hamburgers!

Moses gets all huffy and throws down the rocks he wrote the rules on and breaks them. The Wiz is pretty peeved about the whole cow worship thing too so he makes everyone confused about how to walk a straight line and causes them to wander around on like 40 acres of desert for 40 years. They finally find the place they're supposed to live but Moses doesn't get to live there because The Wiz is fickle like that.

To Be Continued...

So that basically wraps up the Old Testament and the whole Jewish thing. In the next segment I'll break down the New Testament and the story of this Jesus fellow.

INTERLUDE (PART 1)

Very much like a pie, the Bible doesn't add up to much without some filling. But unlike a pie, the Bible's filling is made of crazy.

The Tragic Protagonist

Let's go back and fill in a bit of the miscellaneous details of the story starting from the beginning. If you'll recall there was that talking snake bit back in part one of this series. Well it turns out that The Wiz made a bunch of minions named angels before he made people and some of those minions felt like The Wiz was a real egotistical and self-centered asshat. One of those angels was this dude Lucifer who was the lead guitarist for The Wiz's private metal band that played night and day in his golden mansion in some alternate dimension until one day Lucifer decided to go for a solo career. This makes The Wiz super pissed and he vows that Lucifer will never get another gig in the golden mansion again. So The Wiz kicks Lucifer out of the mansion and tells him that one day he's gonna set all of Lucifer's shit on fire like a jealous ex-girlfriend. So that's when Lucifer or one of the angels that joined Lucifer's new band did the whole talking snake thing that totally tricked eve into screwing the pooch and eating the fruit.

In all fairness, if you've ever read the Bible you know that The Wiz's contracts can be a bit brutal to adhere to. Although he does only charge 10% which is rather low in the industry.

The Gambler

After all that nastiness with the flood, The Wiz develops a gambling habit. During this time Lucifer bets with The Wiz that this guy named Job who is a huge fan of The Wiz will totally ditch The Wiz if he stops treating the guy all special. So The Wiz takes the bet and destroys all of Job's shit and murders his family with fireballs and shit. Then he gives him boils on his whole body, but Job is still a total fanboy for The Wiz.

Now, there wasn't really anything at stake in this bet and The Wiz and Lucifer just go their separate ways. Meanwhile Job is left broke and homeless and all his family is dead and never to be heard from again.

Tada! Now you're an imbecile Job!

It's All Greek to Me

After the flood folks are calm for a while, but then these people in this place called Babel build a stairway to heaven (that golden mansion in another dimension The Wiz lives in). But a stairway wasn't that feasible, so they built a giant tower instead. The Wiz saw this and was pretty upset, because he's strongly against illegal immigrants. So he destroys the tower and makes everyone speak different languages so they'd be too confused to try and build another stairway to heaven.

This Wiz guy is sounding more and more like a conservative Republican as this story progresses. No wonder the Koch brothers are so fond of this dude.

Foreskins and Other Penis Problems

So The Wiz supposedly tells Abraham to cut the tips off of everyone's penises one day which he makes a mandatory thing for any of his descendants to do. Apparently The Wiz thinks the best way for Jews to distinguish themselves from others is to mutilate their genitals. I can only assume that it was common for men to introduce themselves to others by flashing their dongs at each other making this mutilation of the penis a very good identifier.

Poof! Part of your penis is gone! (That's one of the worst

tricks yet!!)

While Abraham is dragging the Jews around in the middle of nowhere, one of his friends named Lot is kicking it in this town called Sodom. Apparently this town was full of "the gays" and The Wiz was super homophobic. So The Wiz sends a couple minions to Sodom to let the folks know that He's not cool with butt sex. So the minions stop in at Lot's house to let him know that The Wiz was fixing to lay the smack down on Sodom. But a couple guys hear about the minions being at Lot's house and they gather outside and start catcalling the minions. Lot is such a fanboy for The Wiz that he tries to keep the minions from getting molested by these sex crazed gay dudes that he tries to bribe them by offering to let them ravage his daughter in whatever way they please. The dudes outside remind Lot that they are totally into penises and the whole sodomy thing, and Lot's daughter just doesn't get their motors running. This whole mess totally pisses off The Wiz who tells Lot to get the hell out of Sodom before The Wiz starts raining fire onto the city. Lot boogies out of there but his old lady looks back at Sodom and The Wiz says, "Abracadabra! Now you're a pillar of salt!" Because The Wiz knows you've gotta keep your pimp hand strong.

Yada Yada Yada

From here the book just drags on and on about the descendants of Abraham. We see Abraham has a kid named Isaac who then has a kid named Jacob. Jacob gets into a pissing match with his brother Esau. At some point Jacob asks The Wiz for help and so The Wiz put on a human costume and comes to earth. The Wiz sees Jacob walking through the woods and jumps out of the bushes at him. They start wrestling and The Wiz is getting his ass handed to him on a platter, so he uses his wizard powers to dislocate Jacob's hip. But Jacob is still whooping the shit out of him so The Wiz calls uncle and Jacob is like, "What's your name punk?" But The Wiz tries to be all aloof about it and gives him some garbled existential nonsense.

Later Jacob has midlife crisis and changes his name to Israel. He has twelve sons and one is named Joseph. Jacob is especially fond of Joseph and makes him a tie-dyed poncho. His brothers get jealous and sell him into slavery, but Joseph claims he can interpret dreams and ends up working for a bunch of different dudes in Egypt. This one guy's wife accuses him of getting frisky with her and he gets tossed into a dungeon. But the pharaoh at the time has some dreams about cows and shit and no one can interpret them. So one dude tells pharaoh about Joseph and Joseph says, "Pharaoh dude, I can totally get The Wiz to tell me what the dreams mean!" So pharaoh tells Joseph the dreams and Joseph says, "The Wiz told me the dreams mean you should put me in charge." So pharaoh does that...

Poof! Now you're a king! (Even The Wiz is impressed with that one)

So eventually Joseph's brothers show up and so does Jacob. Yada, yada, yada. A new pharaoh takes over and makes the Jews slaves, and we're back to Moses. Some other stuff happens after Moses and we'll touch on those in the final interlude.

THE BIBLE IN A NUTSHELL (PART 2)

The unbelievable tale of The Wiz continues! We've got rape, betrayal, and even more murder to come.

Forward

Our tale picks up many years after Moses leads the Jews around in circles for forty years. They found their special place and Jews are pretty well known.

Artificial Insemination

So Moses got his people out and they built this place called Jerusalem where they worship The Wiz. Several generations go by with The Wiz ordering genocide in his name and having a rather good time of it. Finally The Wiz thinks it's time for an image makeover. So to do this The Wiz uses magic to rape a Jewish virgin girl and implant himself in her body as a baby. This girl named Mary is now impregnated by The Wiz with The Wiz. Some guys hear about this and follow a star to see the birth of the baby Wiz. The baby pops out and Mary says, "We better name you Jesus instead of calling you The Wiz because people might find that weird."

The baby is born in a barn because they were traveling and the hotel had no vacancies. Those guys who were following the star find this baby and give him some gifts of gold, incense, and some oil. And then everybody just does whatever for about 13 years until Jesus starts preaching to priests in a temple. Then another 15 years or so pass without too much fuss and we find Jesus as an adult.

Soapbox Hero

So Jesus is an adult now and he sets out on the mission of trying to make people love The Wiz again. To do this, Jesus invokes super Wiz powers and starts doing magic. He makes a bunch of fish appear out of nowhere and he heals some sick people by putting his hands on them, which I must assume is possible through super Wiz antibodies he spreads through contact. During this time Jesus meets a guy named John the Baptist who likes to splash water on folks and John sees Jesus and says, "Hey... Aren't you that guy?", to which Jesus replies, " Why don't you splash some water on me too." So John runs around and tells everyone that he met that guy from the thing that those people mentioned that one time.

Of course Jesus, being the physical embodiment of a narcissistic extra-dimensional wizard, doesn't do too good without some minions. So Jesus picks up some random dudes on the way who he asks to give up all their stuff and leave their families and come live the hobo life with him. These guys think this sounds awesome and they all pal around for about 3 years or so. Jesus runs around and tells folks how awesome The Wiz is and does some more magic. He feeds hungry folks some bread and fish because they were out in the middle of nowhere and Jesus is a bit long in the tooth. But there isn't enough for everyone so Jesus says, "Alakazam!", and suddenly the endless buffet was born into existence.

Enema of the State

Among some of the things Jesus did were also some subversive acts against the Jewish and Roman officials such as to walk into a temple and beat the crap out of merchants and money changers. He also stopped some townsfolk from stoning a promiscuous woman to death, which was the law and custom at the time. He even took some time to practice his necromancy skills and raised two people from the dead! POOF! Now you're a zombie! Helluva trick!

Jesus' shenanigans were short lived though, because this asshole named Judas would soon turn him over to the Romans. Before that however, Jesus and his crew sit down for a late lunch and Jesus picks up a hunk of bread and says, "Hey guys, I'm gonna use magic to turn this bread into my body and if you don't mind a bit of cannibalism and you eat it you'll live forever." So the guys all do and then Jesus picks up some wine and says, "By the way, you've got to wash it down with my blood too." So everyone pigs out on Christ Crackers and Jesus Juice.

A while later they're all out doing their thing and Judas kisses Jesus on the cheek and Jesus is like, "I knew you were playing for the other team Judas!" The kiss was actually a signal to the Romans to know who Jesus was because all Jews looked the same to them - bunch of racists. So they capture Jesus and put him on trial and Pontius Pilate asks the people what Jesus did to which everyone is just like, "He's a dick! Kill him!" But Pilate says, "I'm not sure what he did but we'll kill him if you want. We were just gonna let him go, but you seem to want us to let this murderer go instead."

So Jesus is savagely beaten and then nailed to a tree. All that asswhooping really gets Jesus confused and he asks himself why he has forsaken himself to which he gives himself no reply and proceeds to die. Let us not forget however that Jesus is actually The Wiz and so he's a necromancer. So after being dead three days Jesus performs his most awesome trick yet and.... POOF! Jesus is now a zombie. Try to top that Penn and Teller!

To Be Continued...

In our final installation, our story wraps up with a few appearances of zombie Jesus and his band of merry hobos continuing to recruit new members to the cult of Christ. Oh.... and there's a dragon too!

INTERLUDE (PART 2)

This is a deep-dish pie, and we've got just a bit more filling before we reach the crust again.

A Major Case of Whiplash

So apparently The Wiz failed to tell the people who already lived on the land where The Wiz had planned for the Jews to live anything about this foreclosure. Instead of giving them a fair ninety days to vacate the premises, The Wiz tells the Jews to just bust in and murder everyone. The Jews have trouble doing this in a timely fashion, so The Wiz makes the sun stop moving so the Jews can complete their attempted genocide in just one day.

A quick note is necessary here because as far as science is concerned, the only way to stop the sun in the sky would be to stop the rotation of the earth. This would mean instant death for everything on earth, but we must remember that we're dealing with an extra-dimensional wizard. The Wiz isn't beholden to physics!

The Wiz is really a swell guy once you get to know him and if he isn't trying to murder you or have you murdered.

Splitting Hairs

Times are crazy and this one dude named Samson has grown out some killer dreadlocks. The Wiz thinks this hairdo is totally dope, so he makes Samson super strong because dreads are super awesome. The Wiz tells Samson that if he ever cuts his hair The Wiz is gonna pull Samson's man card and take all his strength. So Samson starts dating this chick named Delilah and he thinks things are getting serious so he tells her about how The Wiz made him super strong because dude loves the dreads. But Delilah is actually a trifling ass skank and she tells the other dudes that if they shave Samson's killer ass dreads that he'll turn into a total wuss. So those guys shave Samson's head and The Wiz takes Samson's super strength for falling victim to a drama queen. The people in the town have Samson on display and are teasing him and shit so Samson sends The Wiz a telepathic message and asks for an assist. The Wiz is like, "Why the hell not?", and gives Samson his powers back. Samson then proceeds to push over the support pillars for the building they're all hanging out in and drops the roof on everyone's heads.

Poof! Now we're all corpses!

The Bigger They Are...

The Jews have kings in charge of them after Moses and the whole establishment of Israel thing. One of the kings named Saul is having trouble dealing with a race of giants and this dude named David chimes in and says, "I've got this". He's basically still a kid and these other guys bring in this extra-large giant named Goliath. David picks up a rock and puts it in this thing called a sling. He spins it around a few times and then releases one end sending the rock into Goliath's skull and peals his muffin cap back for him.

I make da bodies... I don't erase da bodies!

The Chronicles of Ridiculous

After the whole Moses thing there are a bunch of chapters that chronicle the life and times of the Jews. For the most part these are chapters detailing all the war crimes committed by the Jews while they sought to establish Israel. The basic gist is murder, burn, rinse, and repeat. This goes on for well over a thousand years of building temples, burning temples and general slaughter of as many men women and children as can be found in the region.

It's been about 2,000 years since all that began and we can see that it still continues to this day with no end in sight. It's not much in the way of a magic trick, but as a testament to stubbornness, delusion, and cognitive dissonance it's second to none.

More Royal Cream Filling

There were some more kings and more murder and somewhere in the mix we learn that iron is like kryptonite to The Wiz, so if you ever find yourself on his bad side just get yourself an iron chariot and you're in good shape.

The Jews procreate like rabbits and just conquer everything around. They continue playing this tedious game called burny burny cut cut with all the people around them, especially these folks called Palestinians. The whole region is just covered in blood and guts and everyone is fighting and killing each other as the Jews progress through a procession of warrior kings.

Daniel and the Vegetarian Lions

Eventually the Jews aren't hot shit any more and everybody is worshipping all sorts of weird cosmic wizards. So this one guy named Daniel tells this king that the wizards he's worshipping are total bullshit. So the king says to prove it and Daniel shows the king that the wizards he's worshipping are fake and that the priests who claim to be employed by those wizards are actually just robbing the king. But this just pisses the king off and he throws Daniel in a den of lions. Unbeknownst to the king The Wiz had cast a spell on those lions and made them vegetarians. This saves Daniel's ass, but it's not very cool for the lions whose teeth and digestive system aren't well equipped to handle broccoli.

I Can't Eat Another Bite!

Okay, the rest of this crap leading up to Jesus is just more kings and more bloody rampage. Honestly I've had all of that crimson filling I can stand to ingest, and I imagine you have too. Luckily for us the New Testament is low on filler and there isn't anything to add here that is pertinent to the story.

In the final part Peter Dinklage rides in on a dragon and burns everything down... Well, maybe no Dinklage, but the dragon is totally coming!

A Note from the Author

These interlude pieces are not really necessary to understand the main storyline. I've offered them here because the stories I chose to highlight play a part in what makes up Christian dogma in many traditional sects. Even in offering these most notable of stories some will still object that I missed certain stories they find to be important. What I've offered here is a stripped down rendering of the most basic ideas one should be familiar with to understand the Bible. If you want to go into greater detail then, feel free to read the actual Bible as I've done many times over.

THE BIBLE IN A NUTSHELL (PART 3)

Every story must have an ending, and while this one isn't even on the same level as **Tolkien's The Hobbit**, *we do have a dragon!*

Forward

Our story concludes with a few sightings of zombie Jesus, the recruitment of a murderer as a saint, and an apocalyptic tale that includes a dragon.

Zombies in the Mist

So Jesus gets tortured and nailed to a tree and then dies, which is apt to happen when someone is viciously beaten and nailed to a tree. But Jesus is actually The Wiz and after three days he's had enough of the being dead thing so he turns himself into a zombie. He walks out of his tomb like he's hot shit, which technically he would be seeing as he can turn himself into a zombie and all, and proceeds to jump out of the bushes and scare the shit out of some folks who knew him before he got nailed to a tree. He also pops in to haunt this guy named Paul who was persecuting the crap out of all the people who believed Jesus was really The Wiz in human form. Paul didn't know Jesus before the whole murder thing so Jesus plays peekaboo with him and when Paul can see through his hands he knows it is zombie Jesus and that he's actually The Wiz.

So Paul runs around telling everyone about this. Of course some of the dudes that had actually palled around with Jesus were also running around trying to recruit Jesusites too. This caused for some confusion and so Paul started writing letters to all the churches and told them to listen to him because he had inside information straight from zombie Jesus' rotting lips, so mostly started just doing what Paul said because zombies are scary as shit and a guy who talks to zombies is double scary. The Wiz gets tired of haunting people as zombie Jesus and goes back to chill out in his extra-dimensional mansion outside of space and time and is never heard from again.

The End?

You would think this was the end, but as with most good movies we've got a sting after the credits.

As it turns out The Wiz had one more trick to do before ghosting out stage left. For his finale, The Wiz decides to make this guy named John who lives on an island named Patmos have a piss your pants night terror in which he describes the end of the world. In this nightmare The Wiz shows John these seven scrolls and tells him, "I'm gonna open these like it's a game show and each time I do horrible stuff is gonna happen." To which John replies, "What the hell is a game show?" (Or at least he should have). So The Wiz describes all the horrible shit he's gonna do including plagues and famine and then a dragon shows up (meanwhile we still wait for George R.R. Martin's dragons to show up). The Wiz tells John that he's going to give his evil twin control of the earth for like a thousand years to do whatever he wants too.

John is thinking this all sounds pretty grim, but then The Wiz tells him the up side. He tells John that all the people who worship The Wiz get to come live at his house in some other dimension after they die, but anyone who doesn't worship him is going to be sent to a dimension made of fire and be tortured for eternity.

No Seriously... The End

So that's the Bible in a nutshell, and even in three parts it's still much shorter and easier to understand. There will be critics who say that this is simply too reductionist in nature to convey the supposed nuances of the Bible and I won't argue in opposition to that. The honest truth is that if we seek to see a deeper meaning in any text we'll likely find it. So it may be true that within the Bible one can find deep philosophical ideas, but the same can be said for a Dr. Suess book.

Reductionism of this nature serves a very valuable purpose however and that is to make a point. The point I've tried to make here is that if you reduce something down to its simplest form and it seems ridiculous, then you should dig deeper into its veracity.

To really highlight this, I want to offer you another reductionist story:

Once there was a boy who went to the theater with his parents and afterwards they were mugged. During the mugging the boy's parents were shot and killed. His parents were rich and he inherited a fortune. When he grew up he used that money to build a suit of armor and vehicles he used as a vigilante to stop criminals.

Maybe you know the backstory of Batman and so you know that story isn't a factual tale. However in its simplest form the story of Batman's inception is actually far more believable than the Bible in its simplest form. The only reason people buy the Bible story is because piled onto a simple story about a space wizard is all this other fluff to try and make it look like it has more substance than it really has. But if you strip away the fluff and say it straight you can see it for what it is.

A Note from the Author

I hope you've enjoyed this blog series, however I want to

make something clear. This is not a comprehensive and in depth dissection of the Bible. It is for all intents and purposes a cliff notes version written with a touch of humor. If you are honestly looking for a comprehensive dissection of the Bible, I highly recommend reading any one of the many books by author and theologian Bart Ehrman.

Some may say this was merely blasphemy, and to them I say, "It's been a blast for me too."

EXTRAS & DELETED SCENES

No boxed set is complete without some extras. So here are some alternate endings and deleted scenes!

Alternate Ending

If you thought the original Bible was crazy, you haven't seen anything yet because we've got Bible plus! **Now with aliens!**

Joseph Smith wasn't the first modern prophet to claim an extra special relationship with The Wiz, but he was one of the best. Apparently Smith was contacted by one of The Wiz's minions and told to go dig up some golden tablets. So he does, although no one else sees these tablets, and he tells a buddy to take dictation while Smith deciphers this supposed magic Wiz language with some magic rocks in a hat.

Smith's dictation buddy takes home his notes and tells his wife about the whole thing. She immediately starts calling him a dumbass because the whole thing just reeks of bullshit. So she reads the notes and tells her husband to go back and tell Smith that he lost the notes and get him to retell the story. The dictation buddy does as his wife says and Smith calls him a girl brains and says, "Fuck it. I'll just do this other tablet." Smith sticks his head in the hat again and starts jibber-jabbering about how The Wiz is actually an alien and that Jesus and Lucifer are brothers. These alien god folks all have like 800 wives and they have planets all to themselves to just make babies all day every day.

So if Mormons wear special underwear and convince women that dudes should marry and start families with as many women as they want, they'll get a heaven planet with even more wives after Jesus comes and destroys this shithole.

Deleted Scenes: Apocryphal Texts and Gnostic Gospels

There were a great many stories that were made for the Bible that just didn't make the final cut. In the following section I'll tell you about three of my personal favorites.

<u>The Gospel of Mary Magdalene</u>

This is a rather incomplete text as many apocryphal texts are. There are two very interesting quotes from this text however that are worth mentioning.

The first is this: *"I have left no commandment but what I have commanded you, and I have given you no law, as the lawgiver did, lest you be bound by it."*

It's easy to understand why the editors didn't want this one included in the final cut. It might undermine their authority in making all kinds of laws in the name of The Wiz.

Secondly, in the last bit of this text Mary is asked by Peter to tell all the apostles whatever secret shit Jesus told her. So she tells the guys and Peter has a freaking fit, calling her a lying piece of trash. But then Levi puts Peter in his place by saying: *"Peter, you are always irate. Now I see that you are contending against the woman like the adversaries. But if the Savior made her worthy, who are you to reject her? Surely the Savior knew her very well. For this reason he loved her more than us. And we should rather be ashamed and put on the Perfect Man, to form us [?] as he commanded us, and proclaim the gospel, without publishing a further commandment or a further law than the one which the Savior spoke."*

Apparently Levi wasn't cool with that misogynistic shit the other apostles were putting out there. Unfortunately for Christianity the apostle Paul, formerly Saul, was not too female friendly and his version of the story makes up the largest portion of the New Testament.

The Gospel of Thomas

This is a collection of supposed quotes from Jesus just given for the reader's thoughts. Some of my favorites include:

"Jesus said, "If those who lead you say, 'See, the Kingdom is in the sky,' then the birds of the sky will precede you. If they say to you, 'It is in the sea,' then the fish will precede you.
Rather, the Kingdom is inside of you, and it is outside of you.
When you come to know yourselves, then you will become known, and you will realize that it is you who are the sons of the living Father. But if you will not know yourselves, you dwell in poverty and it is you who are that poverty."

"Jesus said, "I have cast fire upon the world, and see, I am guarding it until it blazes.""

However, my absolute favorite is this little gem:

"The disciples said to Jesus, "We know that You will depart from us. Who is to be our leader?"

Jesus said to them, "Wherever you are, you are to go to
James the righteous, for whose sake heaven and earth came into being."

That one kind of undermines Peter and Paul having a claim to be the leader of the church body.

The Gospel of Judas

They say that there are two sides to every story, however given human nature I'd say that's an overly conservative estimate of how many different versions of any story we'll find. Nevertheless, if all we have is one side of the story it's hard not to form a biased opinion.

In the common Bibles of all Christian sects there is a consensus that Judas was a piece of shit traitor who sold Jesus out for some gold in a sack. But many people haven't heard Judas's side of the story. In this text Judas tells about how Jesus told him secret shit and how Judas was actually super special. Jesus tells Judas that he is supposed to sell Jesus out to those haters and that it's all part of The Wiz's grand plan.

My favorite lines from this choppy but interesting text are:

"But you will exceed all of them. For you will sacrifice the man that clothes me. Already your horn has been raised, your wrath has been kindled, your star has shone brightly, and your heart has been hardened"

These dudes really knew how to make Jesus out to be quite the poet at times!

If you'd like more information about gnostic and apocryphal biblical texts, just follow this link: http://sacred-texts.com/chr/apo/index.htm

A FINAL THOUGHT FROM YOUR RESIDENT HERETIC

As I've read this book again and again it plays out in my head as I've given it to you here. There's no sugar coating and no toying with your emotions with philosophical metaphors. All that is presented here is bad fiction. And in the end that's all the Bible is. It's bad fiction.

But many people out there have never heard the story laid out like this. They've been given the hard-nosed indoctrination that was drilled into their parents before them. They were told all their lives that this book of horrible fiction was actually the facts of real life. They think The Wiz is a real dude and that all these crazy tales really happened. But if this blog series was their first introduction to Christianity, they almost certainly would never simply assume it was factually true.

I hope all you heathens enjoyed my offering of *The Bible in a Nutshell*, and I hope you had a few laughs along the way.

ATHEISTING 101

10 Steps to Proper Atheisting

Atheisting 101
10 Steps to Proper Atheisting

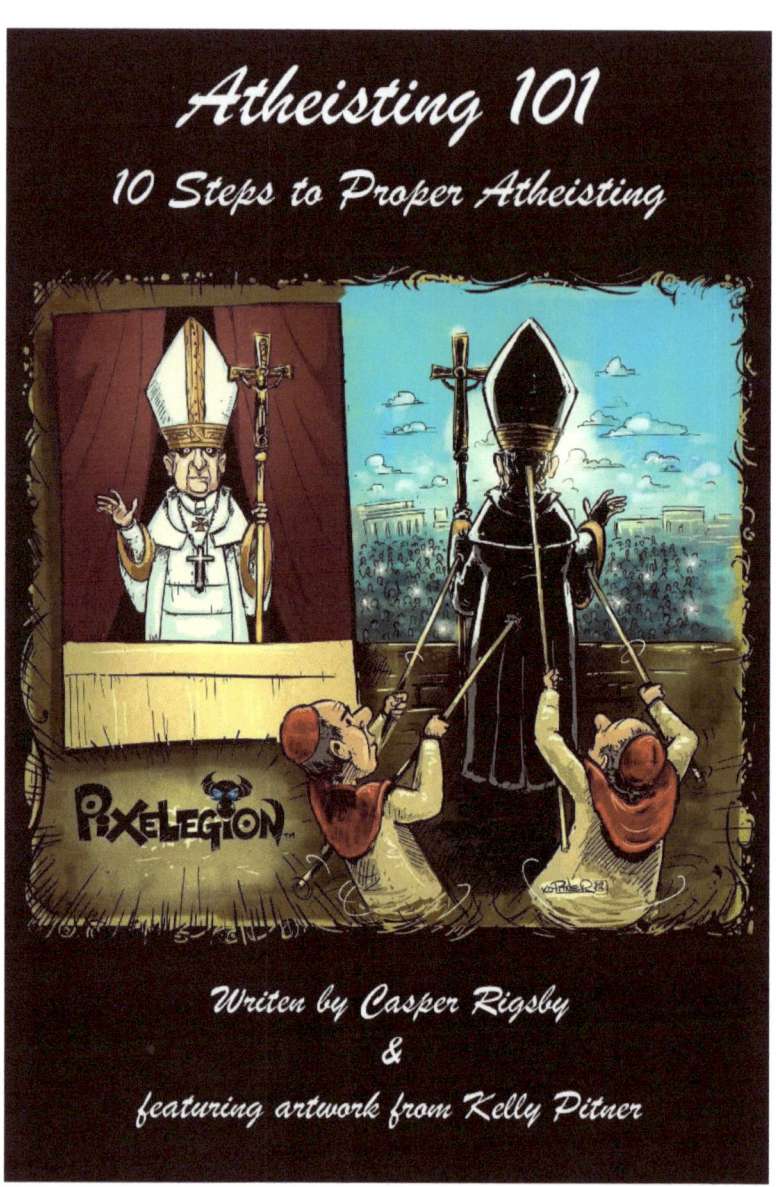

Writen by Casper Rigsby
&
featuring artwork from Kelly Pitner

INTRODUCTION

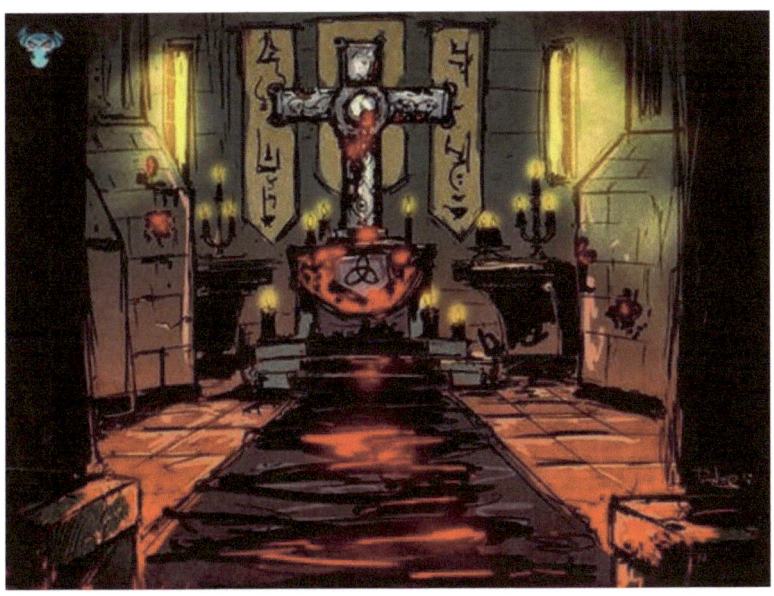

In this short and easy to understand guide you'll learn all about atheism and how you should be *atheisting*. I'll discuss the 10 basic rules of atheisting and how to follow them properly, as well as the reasoning behind these rules. Many of them may seem silly, however these steps have been around for many generations and following them is the only way to be a true atheist.

So without further delay, here are the ten steps to proper atheisting!

PART 1

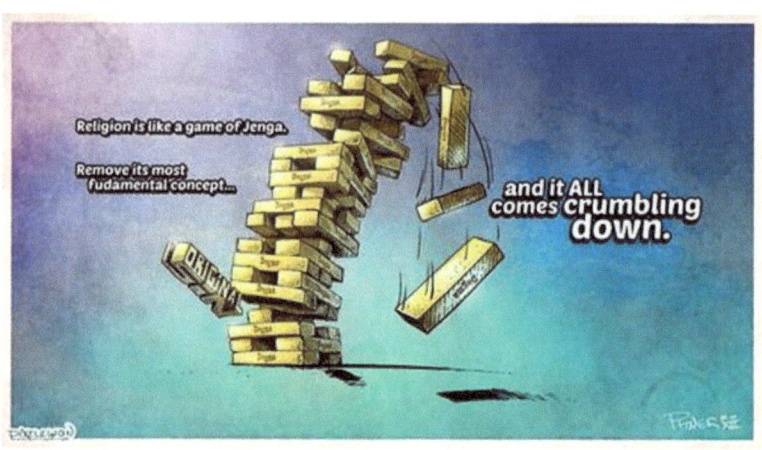

The ten step process.

STEP 1: DON'T BELIEVE IN GODS

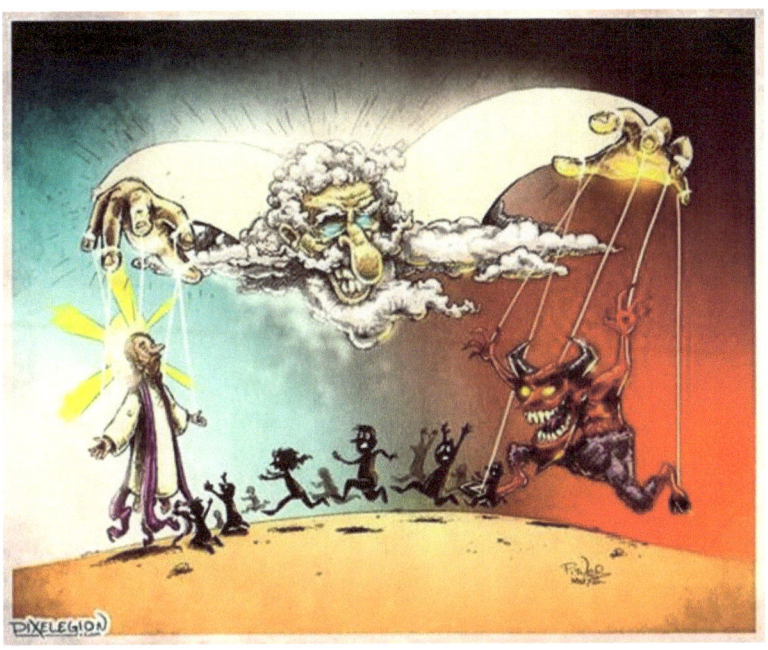

This is the first and most important step to atheisting. If you believe in gods or deities then you are failing entirely at atheisting. It is the golden rule of atheisting, so to speak.

No gods allowed! Period.

Now some may ask, "But Casper, what if I don't believe a god exists, but I also admit that I can't prove one doesn't exist? Doesn't that make me an agnostic?" The answer to that is yes, but if you don't believe in a god then you are still an atheist. This is because a gnostic position and agnosticism are an assertion of knowledge, while theism and atheism are an assertion of belief. So, one can be a gnostic theist who says they know god exists and believe in god. Or you can be a gnostic atheist who claims to know that no god exists and doesn't believe in a god. And then there are agnostic theists and atheists, who both claim to have no knowledge as to be assured that a god does or doesn't exist, but the agnostic theist believes that one does exist and the agnostic atheist does not believe a god exists. So, using the term agnostic as a general label really doesn't mean anything because it doesn't address your belief or lack thereof.

The bottom line is that anyone who does not believe in the existence of god is an atheist by definition. However, there are many people who don't like to wear that label of atheist because of the negative connotations it carries. In the next 9 steps we'll discuss those negative connotations a bit and why people have such a poor view of atheism in general.

STEP 2: WORSHIP SATAN

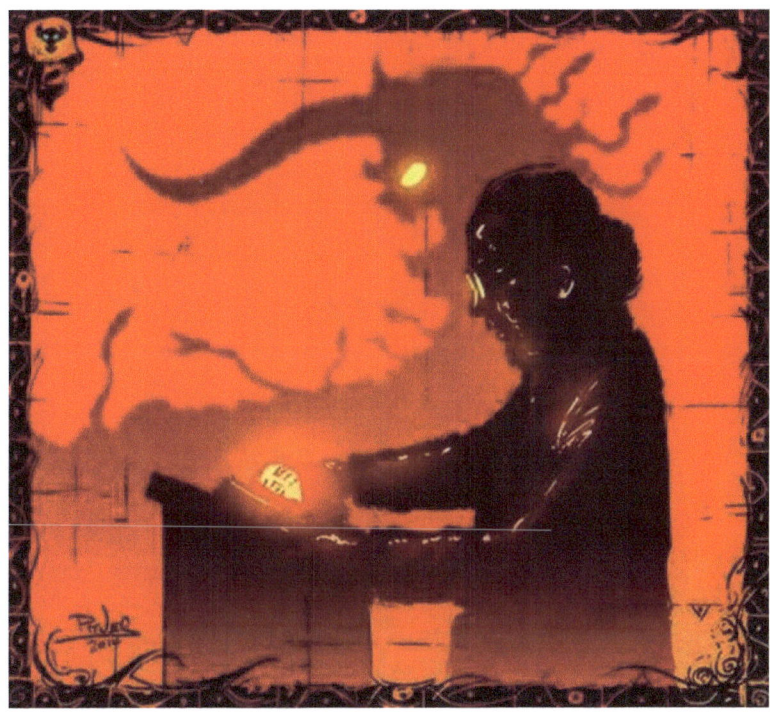

Do you remember how you aren't supposed to believe in gods or deities if you're an atheist? Well, put that aside and worship Satan anyway. This likely seems counterintuitive, but as you'll see soon it all makes perfect sense.

Now, although Satan is a malevolent deity, you apparently don't even have to believe in his existence in order to worship him. You see, no matter how often I explain to theists that if I don't believe in a god that it must naturally follow that I don't believe in his supposed nemesis either, a great many, Christians especially, still persist that regardless of my disbelief I am still doing exactly what Satan wants me to and so I'm apparently actually fighting for his team. Since the only justification for this idea that these theists can give is, *"because I said so"*, or, *"because my holy book says so"*, no amount of logic and reasoning will sway them from this idea. So, while atheists don't actually worship Satan, we still apparently worship Satan... because potato!

The good news here is that you don't have to actually worship Satan to be an atheist. The bad news is that by being an atheist you worship Satan by proxy, at least according to a great many theists and the bible. Since many believers are going to think you are a devil worshiper no matter what you say, I recommend having some fun with them when you run into these obstinate theists. Make your voice sound like a demon from the movies and start chanting gibberish at them, and roll your eyes back as far as you can for added effect. Or, if you want to keep it a bit tamer, just give them the horns and a hearty "Hail Satan!"*

Now, I should also mention here however that the majority of self-described Satanists are actually atheists who happen to also follow a quasi-religious ideology. Oddly enough, the vast majority of Satanists do not actually believe that Satan exists nor do they worship him in any way. If anything, a Satanist worships themselves or humanity as a whole. I'll admit that this could cause some confusion for theists in regard to the difference between an atheist and a Satanist, but it's really hardly an excuse for their insistence that all atheists worship Satan.

The funny part of all this is that only the theist actually believes in Satan. The atheist finds it even more ridiculous to have an imaginary enemy than we find having an imaginary friend, and even Satanists find the whole thing to be rather silly. In the end this is just the theists' way of saying that if we're not with them that we must naturally be against them. Seems legit.

*DISCLAIMER: While I do advocate messing with stubborn adult theists, I do not advocate this behavior with children. A child's mind is very impressionable and you don't want to give them the idea that this Satan worship thing has any validity. As I said, adults who hold to this mindset are usually too far gone to sway, but we don't want to add to the confusion a child may already have due to their delusional parents.

STEP 3: EAT A BABY

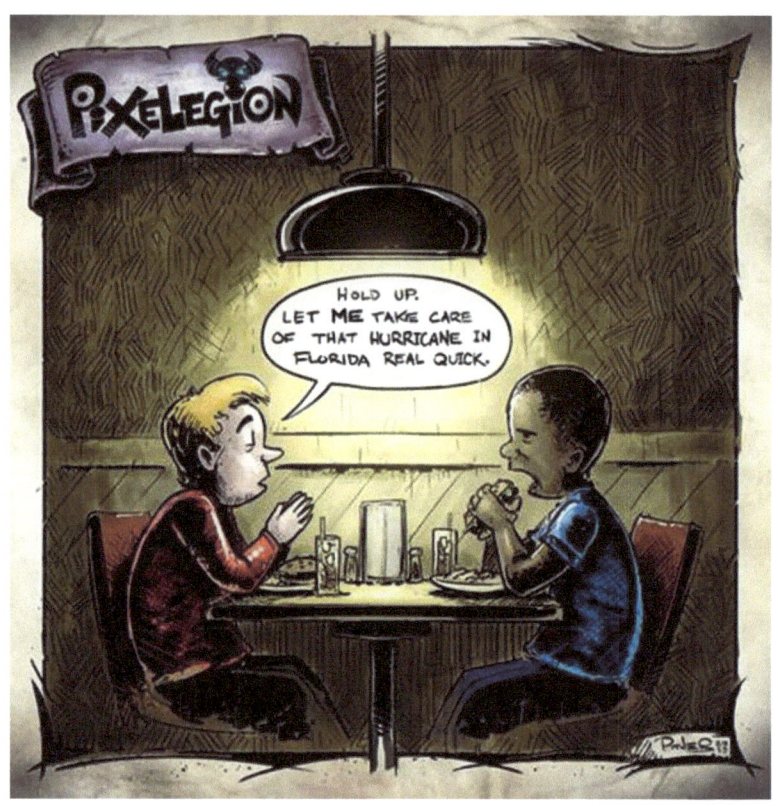

All atheists are required to eat babies. If you're wondering what the hell this has to do with atheism or religion, your guess is as good as mine. However, we know it must be true because a quick Google search turns up all kinds of hits about how atheists eat babies. And as we all know, they can't put it on the internet if it isn't true. So if the internet says we have to eat babies because that's what atheists do, then I recommend having them as a sandwich on banana nut bread with cottage cheese, because if we're gonna get weird and nasty we need to get real weird and nasty.

My only real guess as to why we're supposed to eat babies

is that maybe babies contain Midi-chlorians that will unlock our atheist force powers. Although I've never seen it personally, I once read on the internet that Richard Dawkins once used force lightning to revive Ken Ham after Bill Nye knocked him dead in a debate. When asked why he would revive Ham, Dawkins said, "We're not done ridiculing this fool yet." It's on the internet so it must be true.

While the internet does have all sorts of claims that atheists are baby eaters, there aren't any factual reports of this ever happening. Oddly enough, the most recent case of a person eating a baby was committed by a Christian woman who claims Jesus told her to do it. This just goes to show that theists won't be content until they've taken everything from atheists. I suppose we should just be glad they aren't still taking our lives... oh wait, they still do that too in thirteen countries! My bad.

If you don't find the thought of eating a baby appealing, don't fret. You don't actually have to eat babies either, because as with worshipping Satan, many theists will claim you cat babies no matter what you say. So feel free to have fun with this one too, because if you can't beat them with logic and facts you should at least get some amusement at their expense.

STEP 4: ORGIES! ORGIES! ORGIES!

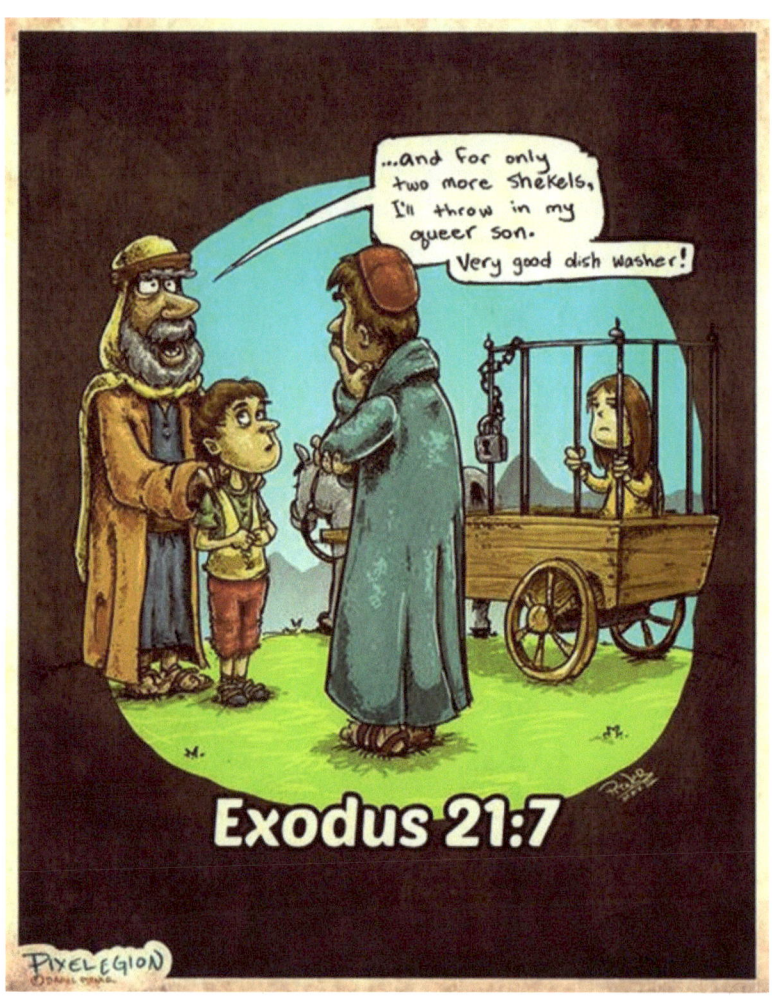

Heathen orgies are a tradition that go way back with atheists and you aren't atheisting at all if you haven't engaged in a heathen orgy yet. According to theists and the internet, the only thing atheists enjoy more than eating babies and worshipping Satan is sexual debauchery. I can't count the number of orgies I've engaged in since becoming an atheist...

only because one can't really count to zero. Even though I haven't engaged in or even been invited to engage in a heathen orgy myself, the internet says they happen all the time so I'm sure it's just a matter of time.

But what if, like myself, you're happily married and devoted to your spouse? Well, as with most of the things theists believe about atheists, no matter what you say they're likely still going to believe you're a whore who *"bumps uglies"* with any heathen you can find. Once again we see that you're still doing something you don't actually do because... potato!

Now, if you're actually looking for these heathen orgies I'll have to burst your bubble and let you know that you probably won't find any. The reality is that heathens aren't any more prone to orgies and sexual debauchery than any other people. Honestly, many of us have very tame sexual appetites and enjoy monogamous relationships. Regardless of the reality however, many theists will always believe that atheists are just running around humping any heathen that moves... ya know... because potato and all.

STEP 5: MURDER & RAPE PEOPLE AS MUCH AS YOU WANT

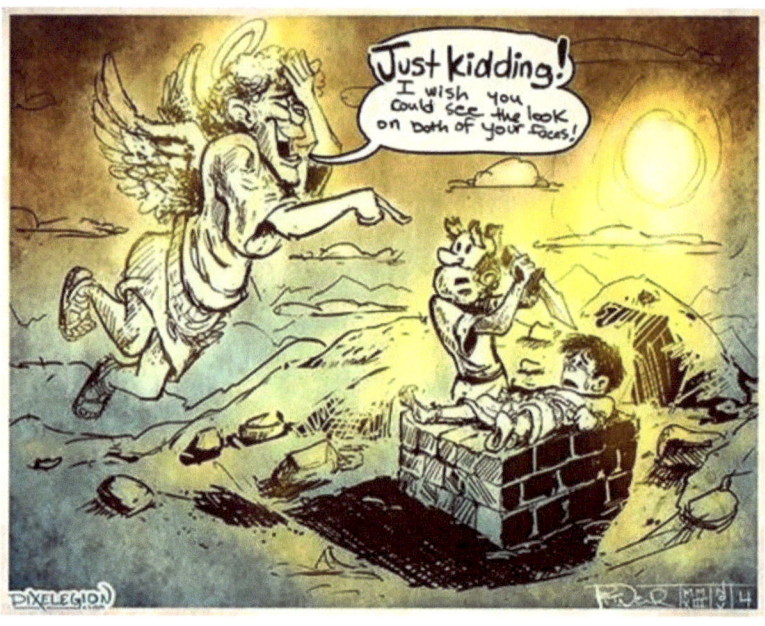

You are now allowed to murder and rape people as much as you want. In all honesty, you can murder and rape as much as you want even if you're a theist. In either case, a person with a compulsion to commit these acts is very likely going to act on those compulsions. Luckily for us, the vast majority do not feel compelled to murder or rape others, or to commit any other actual crimes either. The vast majority of humans don't want to harm or violate others in any way.

We all murder and rape folks just as much as we want to, and as it turns out, for most of us we never really want to do these things at all. I've never murdered or raped anyone because I've never wanted to do that to anyone. However, I'm fairly certain that if I did want to do such a thing that no ancient book nor any current law would stand in my way. Many self-professed Christians have murdered others regardless of the bible or their Christian upbringing, or even the laws of the land which later would be used to hold such people accountable for these deeds.

The real idea the theist is trying to pose in saying we atheists can just murder and rape all we want, is to imply that we have no moral or ethical center or base. The assertion made by most theists is that atheists lack a basis for morality or simply hijack the moral ideas of religion. The theist asserts a base of moral objectivity as given by their doctrines and claims that the atheist can make no morally objective claims. Because he claims we can make no objective claims on moral truths, the theist can then claim that atheists simply act however they want without any moral compass.

You can dispute this all day long and try to explain that your moral compass is just as accurate, if not more so, than theirs because each of us develop our moral standards through society and culture, as well as through a developing understanding of ethics, but such arguments nearly always fall on deaf ears. Even if you were to explain that morality is an evolving concept that grows as our understanding of ethics and logic pushes us ever towards a more equal and justifiable perspective for all humanity, and explain why this is why our ideas on morality cannot be based on 2,000 year old nonsense, and yet, as logical and evidence based as such a position is, it will likely hold no sway with the hardliners of the fundamentalist world. And once again we see that yet another of these steps is merely some nonsense dreamed up by theists which we will simply have to deal with because potato.

STEP 6: WAGE WAR AGAINST CHRISTMAS JESUS

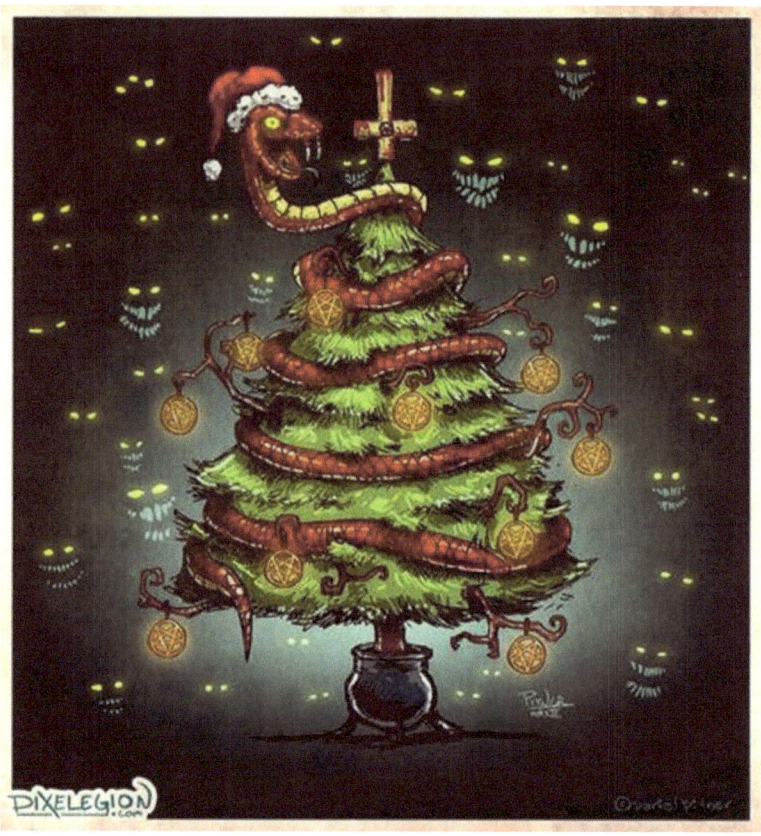

Now, you're probably wondering who this Christmas Jesus is, why you need to wage war against him, and should you choose to wage war against him, how to go about doing that.

First, I suppose I'll address who this Christmas Jesus is. Christmas Jesus is the blonde haired and blue eyed Jesus that evangelical nut-jobs such as Kirk Cameron picture Jesus to be. This Jesus was born on Christmas, is a white dude that looks oddly like the son of an ancient Italian thug, who founded the United States, and who personally wrote the second amendment of the constitution. This Jesus is also known as Raptor Jesus as he is believed to have ridden a dinosaur through Bethlehem and Jerusalem.

This may sound like a foolish thing to fight against, however the only thing you have to do in order to fight this Jesus is to be an atheist. The very act of being an atheist means you hate Christmas Jesus and you're out to destroy him and Christmas. If you actually do want to fight Christmas Jesus you can simply point out to Christians all throughout the holiday season that Christmas was originally a pagan holiday that was hijacked by Christianity and actually has absolutely nothing to do with Jesus or the bible. You get bonus points if you remember to point out the fact that the bible actually explicitly forbids Christmas trees.

I know many of you are probably thinking that no one is stupid enough to actually believe in this Christmas Jesus, however I would remind you that Kirk Cameron just made a movie meant entirely to sell Christmas as a strictly Christian holiday that revolves entirely around Jesus and has been hijacked and misrepresented by "secularists". Because of people like Cameron and his ilk, there actually are quite a few of us atheists who do in fact argue against such idiocy. Although, it isn't much of an argument to simply state the factual truth and point out that what Cameron and the like offer is absolutely insane and not factually correct at all.

STEP 7: WORSHIP RICHARD DAWKINS

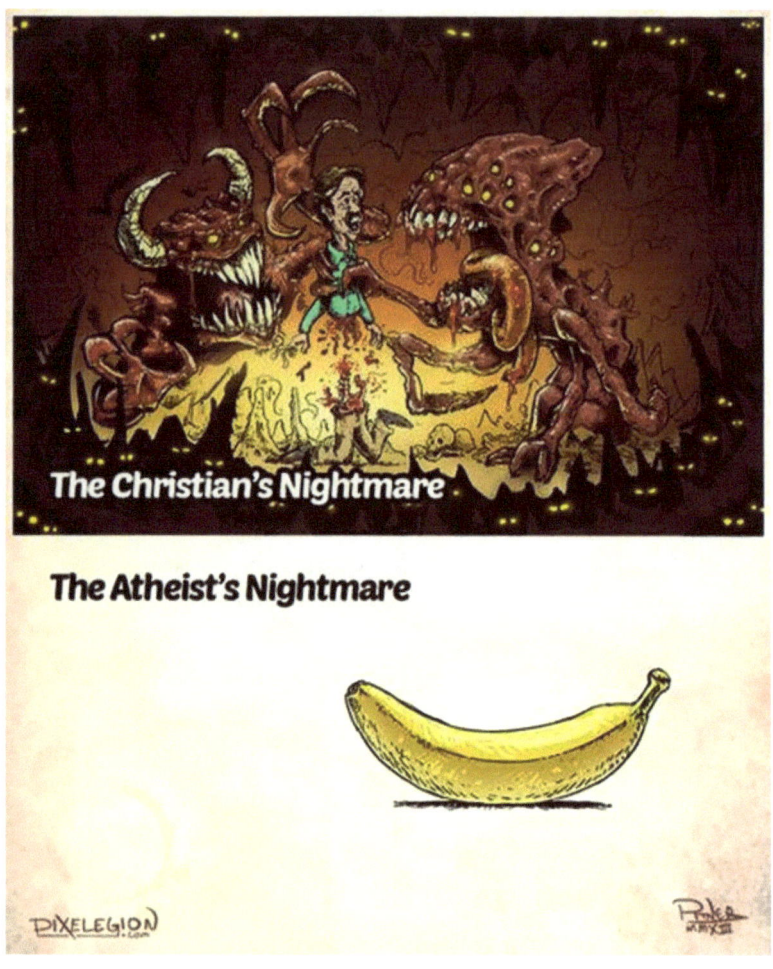

So apparently, Satan is our master and Dawkins is his prophet. This means that as an atheist you must agree with everything Dawkins says ever. This can be one of the most difficult things to do because Dawkins often says some rather socially insensitive things that many atheists don't really agree with at a personal level. One example of this would be the

"Dear Muslima" letter Dawkins wrote. This letter was terribly insensitive to a great many women, so much so that he issued a formal apology for his callousness. But all atheists had to stand behind this act of insensitivity because if we didn't we would lose our atheist card and be excommunicated from the atheist coven. Many atheists did speak out about this and are still trying to get back into good standing with the atheist grand council. Any atheist who doesn't love Dawkins, and the lesser prophets Harris and Krauss, and also the late prophet Hitchens, isn't a "true" atheist.

In all honesty this is absolute nonsense. While many atheists do appreciate the works of those men, we don't all agree with everything they say and they aren't the "leaders" of the atheism. Some atheists aren't fans of one or more of these men at all. Plenty of atheists have strong negative opinions about Dawkins and Harris and Krauss and any other high profile atheist. Those men speak for themselves, as do all atheists.

STEP 8: FREE PHD!

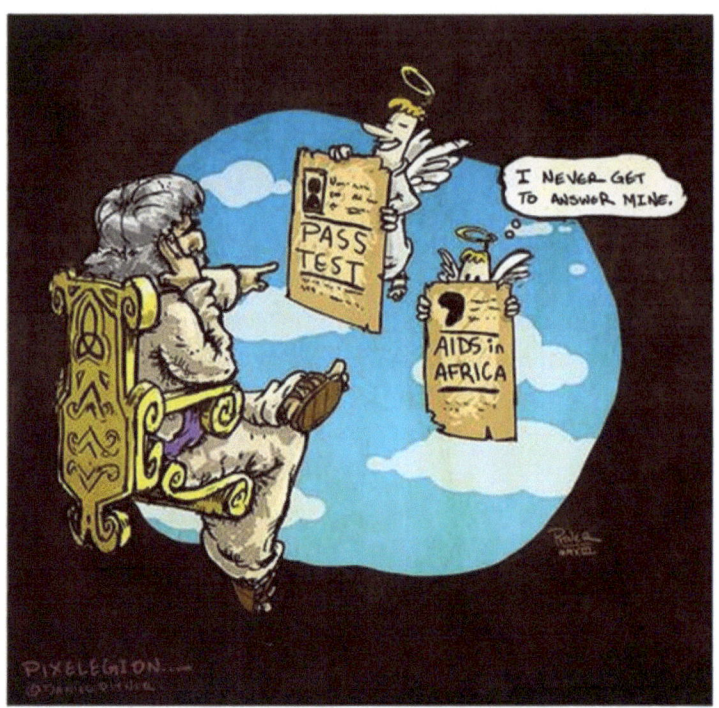

As an atheist, you now have a PhD in evolutionary biology and are required to offer a free college education to any creationist on Facebook, although no matter what you say they won't actually debate any of it.

If Richard Dawkins would have known that all he had to do to become an expert in evolution was to deny the existence of god, he might not have wasted all those years actually learning the subject in school. Luckily for you, I'm giving you the scoop on this little known secret.

By stating that you don't believe in god, your super atheist powers, which are dormant in theists, become active and impart you with a PhD in evolutionary biology. Now, this doesn't mean you'll actually know anything about the topic at all mind you, only that all internet trolls of the creationist variety will act as though you know everything there is to know about the topic. They will also act as though it is now your job to impart them with a free college education on the subject of evolution.

Don't worry about the fact that you don't actually have that PhD however, because no matter what you say to these folks they aren't going to listen. Even if you actually do have a PhD, they aren't going to listen to you. There are a treasure trove of videos on YouTube where one can actually watch entire audiences of people sit in awe as creationists such as Ken Ham explain such nonsense as that dinosaurs and mankind lived side by side, that all dinosaurs used to be vegetarians, and of course that gay marriage leads to bestiality... because nothing says you're an expert in human beings and their origins like some good old fashioned bigotry. Can I get a R'amen!?

So what can you do when you run into these people, and trust me, if you use the internet, especially social media sites, you're going to run into them.

There are at least three options here. First, you can ignore them, which is a fairly sensible option. If you're hot tempered or easily angered, avoidance is actually the best option. It's honestly very hard to keep your composure with these folks, and only those with a great deal of patience should engage these people.

Your second option is to academically engage them. If you're knowledgeable about the subject, then by all means press them with the facts. However, you have to remember that these sorts of debates only serve the audience. If no one is watching, then the exchange is almost entirely pointless. No matter what facts you bring to the table, your opponent is already invested in the notion that you're wrong, and no amount of evidence is going to change that.

The third option, and my personal favorite, is to utilize a mixture of education with sarcasm and light ridicule. I will often give links to educational material attached to a sarcastic or ridiculing remark. For example I might say, "There was a global flood and two of every animal got on the Ark, correct? So how the hell did penguins get to the Antarctic Circle? With the exception of a few remote areas, penguins have never existed anywhere above the equator. And they've certainly never left any sign of ever having lived in ancient Mesopotamia." Followed by a link to facts about penguins. This way, those who do actually want to understand what I'm talking about can look it up, and my opponent just looks like a fool trying to hand off nonsense as fact.

No matter what you choose to do, the important thing to remember is that you're playing pigeon chess. There is no way to "win" the game. No matter how good your argument or what moves you make, the pigeon is going to hop up on the board, knock all the pieces over, shit on the board, and then strut around as if he's won. So what matters is how you play the game, because other people are watching who actually want to learn.

On occasion, the pigeon will give up and fly away, shitting on everything as it leaves. This is called a ragequit, and it's as close to a win as most of us ever get.

STEP 9: EMBRACE REALITY

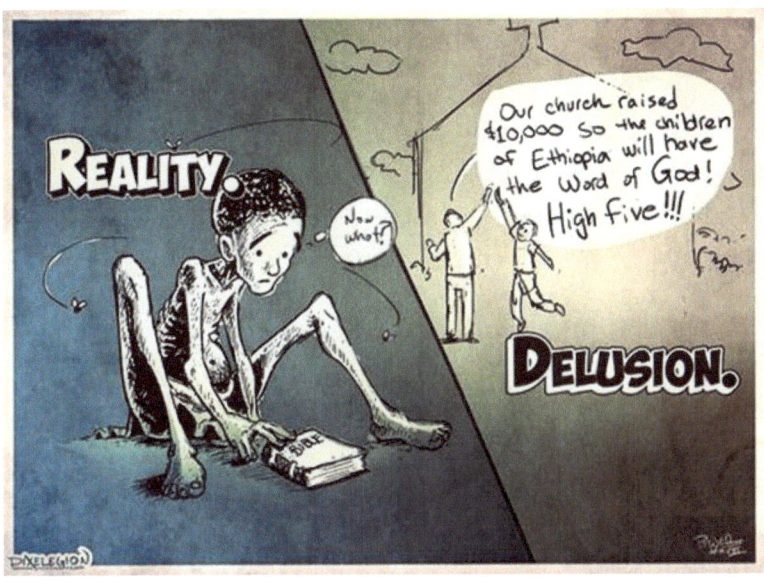

Okay, look. Up until now I've just talked about ridiculous crap that's been borne from the minds of ignorant people. It's at this point that I think we all need to embrace reality a bit.

Atheism gets a bad rap for a lot of reasons and most of those reasons are absolute nonsense. The truth is that atheists are generally very moral people who don't worship, or even believe in, Satan. We also don't think of Dawkins as some prophet. He's just a pretty smart guy who has some pretty good ideas from time to time, but he's wrong quite often as well.

People like Ray Comfort and Pat Robertson are always going to paint atheists in an "evil" light because they don't want their followers to listen to what we have to say. It's much easier to vilify a person and ignore their arguments, than to actually address the arguments. This is especially true when your main argument is, "Hey, but this book says..."

STEP 10: SEE STEP 1

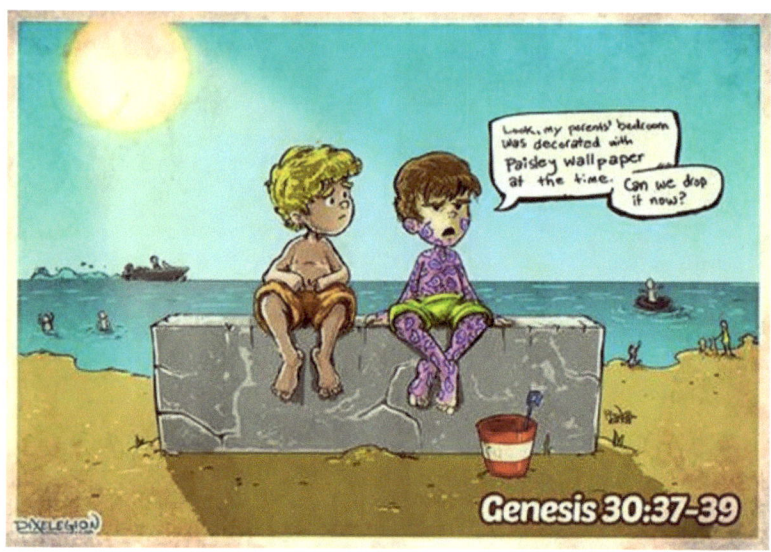

Even though atheism should be the simplest thing ever to understand, it never fails that both believers and those just leaving their beliefs, often ask what atheism is and how one goes about being an atheist. In the end, all I can ever tell them is to see step one here in this guide. Atheism is just a lack of belief in the existence of god. Period. It's so simple a caveman should understand it.

Like any other group out there, when people make generalized assumptions about a group of people, they're almost always wrong. Every atheist is an individual, and the only general consensus between us is that none of us believe in the existence of god.

PART 2

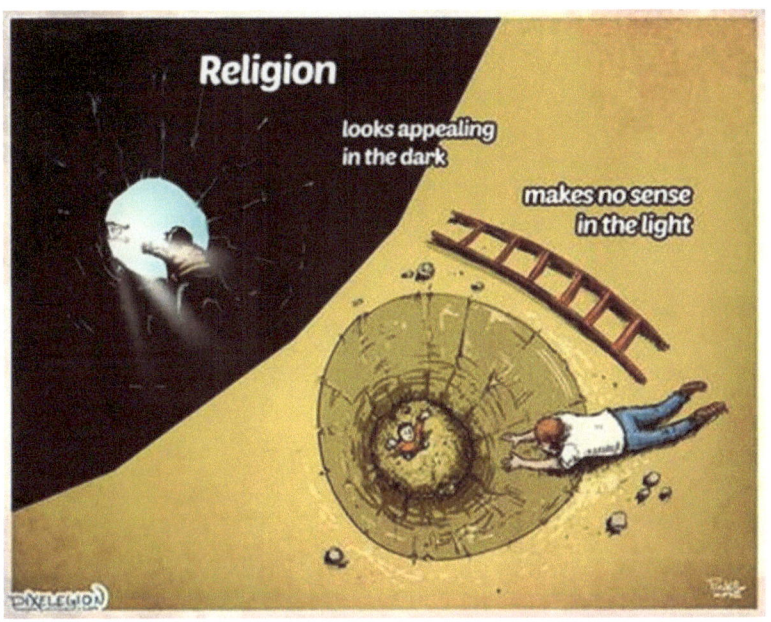

Digging Deeper

The whole first part of this book was simply an attempt to highlight the absurdities and generalizations that atheists deal with on a constant basis. Nearly every atheist who openly admits their position as an atheist has had one or more of these silly ideas thrown at them. Men like Pat Robertson and Joel Osteen have told millions on national television that atheists are just minions of their imaginary enemy named Satan. And no matter how many times we say it, or how we try to explain it, some people just don't understand what utter rubbish those claims are.

Now, if you're a believer and you've always believed one of those silly claims or some other nonsense about atheists, and you're now questioning what atheism is all about if not those things, then please be ready to read and understand what I'm about to say in these next few paragraphs. If you **truly** want to understand what atheism is really all about, then just pay attention to what I'm about to tell you.

Atheism is about one thing, and one thing only. It is the disbelief in the existence of god. It is simply a theological and philosophical position. That's all it is, and that one thing alone is the only true common thread that binds atheists. It's a very loose thread that's able to stretch very well. You can be an atheist and still believe in ghosts. You can be an atheist and still believe in a possible afterlife. Being an atheist only really identifies one singular philosophical position, and certainly doesn't preclude a whole realm of others.

Even so, the atheist worldview tends to draw many of us to very similar conclusions. Because the atheist worldview precludes the idea of a creator who made humans special, and made some humans more special than others, many atheists tend to have strong views on social equality and human rights. When you take away the justification for supposed superiority, it becomes difficult to hold to the notion that all humans deserve equal and fair treatment by all other humans. It becomes a simple matter of what is logically true. If there is no valid reason based on factual evidence to label someone or some group as inferior, then treating them inferiorly is unethical.

This is something that a great many atheists believe and subscribe to, and it is the atheist worldview that led to that conclusion for many of us. There simply isn't any valid logical reason to discriminate or treat anyone unfairly, and so a great many atheists who hold to a strictly logical perspective tend to champion equality and justice for inequality. Even without the belief in god, we know what it is to be good to one another, and the vast majority of atheists act according to that understanding.

For me, the atheist worldview itself can be summed up very simply. What you do is, you take all the ideas that you've always just believed where true because of god and religion, and you replace the idea of god with logic and factual evidence, and then you run through the idea again and see if it logically makes sense. If something only makes sense because god says so, and doesn't make any logical sense, then it just plain doesn't make sense. So for me, the atheist worldview is simply taking god out of the equation, removing that supposedly divine justifier, and then seeing if you can work the equation out logically. When you do this, you'll come to see that logic gives quite a different answer than doctrine and the supposedly divine command of god. The thing you have to understand is that logic can always justify the equation without a special justifier. This means that although we may not like the answer logic gives, logic always gives the true answer.

Embracing an atheistic worldview has completely changed my perspective on countless issues, and does so for many other atheists. From issues of abortion, to gay marriage, we as atheists try to employ logic to assert honest and truthful positions that can be justified by real physical facts. We try to argue from this position and appeal to the superiority of logic and reason over dogma and superstition. We want to spread this idea to as much of humanity as possibly because the idea is good and just. It breeds fairness and equality. It tends towards justice and the betterment of humanity as a whole.

But in the end, what you really need to understand is that I don't speak for all atheists. Neither does Richard Dawkins or Sam Harris, or any other prolific atheist writer or speaker. We have no head of our community and no singular resounding voice. And we don't want one. We all want to be free to have our own ideas, and to agree with some of what others say, and to disagree with other things that same person says. I want every atheist to be able to agree or disagree with me as they wish and to state it as loudly as they want in their own words. If the only thread connecting us is a lack of belief in god, then everything else is fair game.

Be an individual. Think for yourself. Question everything. Let logic and reason and factual evidence be your guide. And, no matter what anyone says, don't ever be ashamed to wear the label of atheist. After all, all that label means is that you don't believe in god, and that's all it will ever mean. Happy atheisting my friends, and I'll see you out there in the social media playgrounds.

A NOTE FROM THE AUTHOR

If you come away from this book having *learned* anything, I hope what you learned is what atheism **is not** all about. I hope you realize it has nothing to do with devil worship or baby eating or heathen orgies. I hope, that in the not too distant future I don't ever have to actually explain to anyone that atheists neither believe in nor worship Satan. It's the twenty first century none of this should need any explanation.

If you enjoyed the art featured here from Pixelegion, please check out their [Facebook](#) page and also their art on [DeviantArt](#). The Pixelegion crew also helps to admin the [God Doesn't Matter](#) Facebook page so come check out our antics there some time!

ABOUT THE AUTHOR

Casper Rigsby is a 38-year-old husband and father who was raised in a Christian home and is the grandson of a lifelong minister. He studied the Bible under his grandfather's guidance as a youth and considered entering the ministry himself but later came to question Christianity and began studying other religions. After years of study and even reviewing Christianity from a far more critical stance, including study of theology at a collegiate level and review of mythological correlations between all religions, he has come to an apatheistic atheist stance that god doesn't matter. He runs an up-and-coming apatheist Facebook page named God Doesn't Matter, was formerly a prominent blogger for the Atheist Republic website and is a strong advocate for loud atheism and apatheism.

Follow Casper on Facebook:
https://www.facebook.com/CasperRigsbyAuthor
https://www.facebook.com/GodDoesntMatter

And on Twitter:
@GodDoesntMatter

www.ingramcontent.com/pod-product-compliance
Lightning Source LLC
Chambersburg PA
CBHW040324220526
45473CB00009B/2555